GRACE AND GLORY

GRACE
and
GLORY

E. L. MASCALL
Foreword by C. P. Collister

Angelico Press

This Angelico Press edition is a reprint
of the work originally published in
1961 by The Faith Press Ltd.
Angelico Press © 2025

Published under license from the
Oratory of the Good Shepherd as owners
of the Mascall literary estate.

All rights reserved:
No part of this book may be reproduced
or transmitted, in any form or by any
means, without permission

For information, address:
Angelico Press, Ltd.
169 Monitor St.
Brooklyn, NY 11222
www.angelicopress.com

Ppb: 979-8-88677-112-1
Cloth: 979-8-88677-113-8

Cover design
by Michael Schrauzer

TO

THE BENTLEY FAMILY

BRYAN AND NINA

ANNE, NICOLAS,

RICHARD AND TERESA

Diligentissime

FOREWORD
to the
Angelico Press edition (2025)

BY C. P. COLLISTER

ERIC LIONEL MASCALL (1905–1993), a leading British theologian teaching at the University of Oxford in the middle of the twentieth century, challenged the rising naturalism blinding philosophers and theologians to the spiritual plane of existence. By the late 1960s, Mascall concluded that this secular interpretation of reality, including its post-Christian anti-metaphysical assumptions, had permeated popular culture to such an extent that "the vast majority of men and women today organize their lives on the assumption that the only realities of which they need to take account are those that are perceived by their senses in the brief span of time that lies between their conception in their mother's womb and their death on the motorway or in the hospital bed."[1] The rejection (or the forgetting) of the Christian understanding of what it means to be human narrows the vision of the modern man. Mascall warns that this naturalistic way of life blinds persons to the eternal and spiritual realms, and causes them to believe "first, that there is nothing after death that we need bother about, neither heaven, hell nor purgatory; secondly, that there is nothing during this life that we need bother about except the things of this world, neither God nor angels nor devils, neither

---

[1] Mascall, *The Christian Universe* (Brooklyn, NY: Angelico Press, 2023), 15.

prayer nor grace nor holiness."² The post-war man feels free from responsibility for his judgments, choices, actions before God, and participation in a spiritual order—either cooperating with God and his angels, or rebelling alongside devils and demons. Finally, he feels free from the belief that his temporal decisions carry eternal consequences.

But all this "freedom" comes at a cost. Prior to the rise of naturalism, Christian men and women believed that humans, made in the image of God, exist for a purpose. Their ultimate aim in this life is to love God and their neighbor. And their final end in this harmonious order of love—should they accept salvation from their dissonant state of sin through redemption in Christ—is eternal union with the triune God and communion of saints. Mascall sees this Christian understanding of the purpose of life under attack, and offers a corrective: "the very people who pour scorn on the picture of heaven as a place where a celestial orchestra performs unending symphonies for the glory of God and the delectation of the redeemed, will in many cases tell you that the most intense delight which they know is that of listening to music."³ Even naturalists, persons who believe that all existence is reducible to the physical and the sensable, long for beauty and order. The voluntarist freedom that modern persons gain by abandoning their Christian faith in God and his purpose for them means loss of hope for an eternal freedom from sin and death in the new heavens and new earth.

In *Grace and Glory*, Mascall turns to St Augustine's *City of God* to recover what it means for persons to hope for eternal life in accord with Christ the Word: "There we shall rest, and we shall see; we shall see, and we shall love; we shall love and

² Ibid., 15.
³ Ibid., 53.

we shall praise. Behold what shall be in the end and shall not end."[4] In a single sentence, Augustine summarizes Christian hope, and in doing so, he explains the ultimate freedom that eludes men and women who live as if nature is all that exists.

In *Grace and Glory*, Mascall insists that "if we are living in the grace of God, heaven is the destination to which our journey is leading us. It is therefore the merest folly for us to behave as if our whole destiny was contained within the limits of this present life."[5] Secularists, whether committed to individualism or collectivism, err in thinking that this worldly happiness, prosperity, and welfare constitute the final end of man. Mascall offers a sobering rejoinder to this immanent framework—"[the final end of persons] is either heaven or hell—either the glad acceptance or the sullen refusal of the beatific vision of the Holy Trinity."[6] This "two-ways" eschatology insists that each person walk the way of life or the way of death, each keeping their gaze directed to God or turning their eyes away from him to fix them instead on lesser goods. The notion that our desires will find rest in the beatific vision troubles theologians of this worldly cast of mind, and Mascall recounts that one such leading ecclesiastic informed him "that he would like to abolish the word 'rest' on tombstones, and substitute the word 'work.'" [7] Mascall finds this to be a naturalistic revision of Christian doctrine, a tendency he opposes in works such as *The Secularizing of Christianity* and *Theology and the Gospel of Christ*.[8] Both liberal individualist and Marxist

---

[4] *Vacabimus et videbimus, videbimus et amabimus, amabimus et laudabimur. Ecce quod erit in fine sine fine* (*The City of God*, Book XXII, ch. xxx).
[5] Mascall, *Grace and Glory* (Harrisburg, PA: Morehouse-Barlow, 1961), 1.
[6] Ibid., 2.
[7] Ibid., Ramsey, "Preface," xvii.
[8] See E. L. Mascall, *The Secularization of Christianity: An Analysis and a Critique* (New York: Holt, Rinehart and Winston, Inc., 1966) and *Theology and*

collectivist err in reducing humans to their economic context and motives, and Mascall believes that such revisions to our vision of the eschaton to fit naturalistic assumptions distort our vision of the New Jerusalem: "Bustle and activity being the characteristics of our age, a superficial mind can suppose that these must be the characteristics of heaven also."[9] Mascall's *Grace and Glory* challenges moderns to recall that God's ways are not our ways (Isaiah 55:8–9).

Secular persons, therefore, need a reorientation to reality that reveals the narrow way of Christ leading to perfect rest in the new heavens and new earth. This narrow way is incorporation into Christ and union with the triune God that allows persons to participate in this eternal rest: "God is changeless, not because He is lifeless but because He is fully active and actual, infinite fullness to which nothing can be added and from which nothing can be lost." And this eternal action of the unchanging God who creates and sustains all things occurs in the personal "Trinity of Father, Son and Holy Spirit, united in one perfect circulation and interchange of Love. Our full possession of this rest awaits us in heaven, but its foretaste is given to us here: 'Grace is a beginning of glory in us.'"[10] The grace of God, given by God in the sacraments, redeems the faithful and prepares citizens of heaven for their eternal rest in the New Jerusalem.

When secular persons try to revise the Christian conception of God as unchanging and blessedness as rest to fit the modern ideal of the human as active contributor to the market or the commune, they challenge the Catholic ideal of devotion in the life of the saint. Mascall rejects the privileging

the Gospel of Christ: An Essay in Reorientation (London: SPCK, 1977).
[9] Mascall, Ramsey, "Preface," *Grace and Glory*, xvii.
[10] Mascall, *Grace and Glory*, 19.

of action over contemplation in Christian devotion: "in contemplative prayer we are not strictly speaking passive, in the ordinary sense of that term, but receptive—receptive of God's own self-contemplation, caught up into God's own life and energized by Him."[11] This paradoxical truth means that many contemplatives took bold and decisive action for the glory of God.[12] The naturalism ascendant in the late-modern West causes many to insist that Christians who focus too much of their attention on eternity or too much of their devotional life on contemplative prayer will fail to "make a difference" for the poor and suffering in this temporal life. By contrast, Mascall argues that Christians who put knowledge, love, and praise of God above all else find that God provides them with the other goods of creation mysteriously offered as a gift (Matt 6:31–33). Seeking God's heavenly kingdom and living on earth as the saints live in heaven brings more spiritual renewal to the fallen world than does living as if this material world matters more than the human *telos* of praising God.[13]

By emphasizing the heavenly citizenship of Christians on pilgrimage in this veil of tears, Mascall does not mean to dismiss the goodness of the creation (nor its capacity to declare the glory of God). He argues, in fact, that "the more we are conscious of the goodness and the beauty of the finite world, the more fully we shall be brought to recognize the infinite and transcendent goodness and beauty of God, provided only—and this is, of course, essential—that we joyfully recognize Him as their source."[14] The creation reflects God's

---

[11] Ibid.
[12] Ibid., 19–20.
[13] The seed of Mascall's argument in *Grace and Glory* originates in his article "The Primacy of Praise" (*Cross Currents* 6, no. 3, 1956: 218–25).
[14] Mascall, *Grace and Glory*, 26.

glory and testifies to his goodness as its creator and sustainer. But because of its contingency and creaturehood, the creation must never be worshiped or confused with God. Mascall maintains the importance of both: giving thanks for the good of the creation, and also avoiding the perils of idolatry and pantheism, as he encourages pilgrims sustained by grace on their journey to glory.

Mascall's guide for pilgrims takes the final state of the blessed, as described by Augustine, as a roadmap to the heavenly city: Christians are to see and to know, to know and to love, and to love and to praise. But how can sinners in a fallen world, the spiritually blind looking for God in a fractured mirror, see God clearly enough to commence this journey? It is the incarnation of God in the flesh that answers this question: "[W]e see God in Jesus. We see Jesus in His saints. And in heaven the whole mystical Body of Christ will gaze adoringly upon the face of the Father through the eyes of Jesus, who is its Head."[15] If we have seen Christ, we have seen the Father (John 14:8) because he is the image of the unseen God (Col 1:15). And Mascall insists that when we gaze on God in Christ with infused charity, we are transformed into the likeness of the one we fix our eyes on. The grace of charity in this life, made possible through the incarnation, death, resurrection, and ascension of Christ, allows the redeemed to see, know, and love God in a grace-filled way that will reach its glorious consummation in the resurrection and new creation.[16]

Among Mascall's books confronting the rise of naturalism and the forgetting of what it means to be human, *Grace and Glory* uniquely elevates the final end of personhood. God

[15] Ibid., 27.
[16] Ibid., 31.

makes men and women to see him: first, they do so through a glass darkly; ultimately, face to face. "In the beatific vision," Mascall reminds us, "we shall be supremely and immeasurably happy, but we shall not be thinking about our happiness. We shall be thinking about God, and that is why we shall be supremely and immeasurably happy."[17] In a secular age, amid the rise of expressive individualism, Mascall reminds his readers that it is in turning our gaze away from the self, and forgetting our pursuit of selfish desires, that we can find our ultimate happiness, a happiness that requires temporal sacrifice. Living for the love of God and neighbor, a life made possible by the gift of God's grace, calls us to the final end of worshiping the blessed Trinity in the new heavens and new earth. And "the sole justification for praising God is that God is praiseworthy. We do not praise God because it does us good, though no doubt it does. Nor do we praise Him because it does Him good, for in fact it does not."[18] The goal of praising God liberates persons from slavery to selfish desire — "praise is thus strictly ecstatic, in the sense that it takes us wholly out of ourselves; it is purely and solely directed upon God."[19] The end of the Christian pilgrimage, made possible through the sustenance of God's grace, is ecstatic union with God and our fellow pilgrims in the communion of saints. This slim book calls Christians to remember that we are strangers in a strange land and citizens of heaven. It is this recollection that empowers us to reflect Christ's light amid the darkness of the fallen world.

---

[17] Ibid., 42.
[18] Ibid., 57.
[19] Ibid.

PREFACE

BY THE ARCHBISHOP OF YORK

A LEADING ecclesiastic said the other day that he would like to abolish the word 'rest' on tombstones, and substitute the word 'work.' I felt the remark to be one more instance of that secularizing of our ideas of religion which is so sadly popular. Bustle and activity being the characteristics of our age, a superficial mind can suppose that these must be the characteristics of heaven also. But the Christian hope, so far from endorsing our mental habits, challenges them sharply, and nowhere more than by telling us that 'rest' is what God has in store for us.

It will, of course, be 'rest' with a difference. 'We shall rest, and we shall see; we shall see, and we shall love; we shall love, and we shall praise. Behold what shall be in the end, and shall not end.' These words in which S. Augustine describes heaven are the theme of this book by Dr. Mascall. He draws out their meaning, and shows how they tell not only of the goal of our destiny, but also of the pattern of Christian life now in this world. If our citizenship is already in heaven, then heaven gives the clue to what we are and what we do to-day.

My gratitude for this book is very great. Here is theology for everyman, like all true theology profound in thought and simple in language. Here is wisdom, drawn from one of the timeless classics of Christian writing, and applied with sympathetic understanding to our own time. Here is one of the doctrines of our faith, often pushed away to the far horizons of our attention, brought vividly near to us. Dr. Mascall's book is a practical vindication of the words of Thomas à Kempis, 'The sons of God standing upon the things that are present, do contemplate the things that are eternal. They look on transitory things with the left eye, and with the right eye do behold the things of heaven.' This book can help us to have both eyes open and alert.

MICHAEL EBOR

CONTENTS

FOREWORD		*page* ix
PREFACE		xvii
I.	Grace and Glory	1
II.	'We shall rest'	12
III.	'We shall see'	21
IV.	'We shall love'	33
V.	'We shall praise'	51
VI.	The Things that are not Shaken	62

I
Grace and Glory

THIS is a book for Christians who are still upon earth, but I have based it upon a sentence in which S. Augustine describes our future life in heaven: 'There we shall rest and we shall see; we shall see and we shall love; we shall love and we shall praise. Behold what shall be in the end and shall not end.'[1] I am not, however, inviting my readers to close their eyes to the things of this world and console themselves for its miseries by reflecting upon the joys that are to come. On the contrary, I want to help them to live their lives upon this earth more joyfully and more fruitfully; I am not advocating any form of escapism. But there are in fact two very good reasons why Christians who are on earth should think about their future beatitude.

The first reason is that, if we are living in the grace of God, heaven is the destination to which our journey is leading us. It is therefore the merest folly for us to behave as if our whole destiny was contained within the limits of this present life. *Respice finem*, 'Look to the end,' is a pagan motto but a very wise one; the only question is what the end may be. For the secularist—and secularism is the dominant note of the civilization in which we live—the end is a this-worldly one, whether it is viewed as my individual

---

[1] *Vacabimus et videbimus, videbimus et amabimus, amabimus et laudabimus. Ecce quod erit in fine sine fine.* (*The City of God*, Book XXII, ch. xxx.)

prosperity and happiness or as the welfare of the human race. For the Christian, it is either heaven or hell—either the glad acceptance or the sullen refusal of the beatific vision of the Holy Trinity. There are, nevertheless, errors about the relation of our ultimate destiny to our present earthly life into which it is only too easy for Christians to fall; we may perhaps best avoid them by recalling that in the Creed the Life Everlasting is spoken of in the closest connection with two other great articles of the Christian Faith, namely the Resurrection of the Body and the Communion of Saints.

'The Resurrection of the Body.' There must be no false spirituality in our attitude, that is to say no suggestion or assumption that Christianity is concerned only with our spiritual part, our 'soul' or 'mind,' and that our bodies and the material objects which nourish and sustain them are outside the concern of religion. Christ has taken, in His Incarnation, not just a human soul but human nature in its fullness, soul and body alike, and in that human body He has risen from the dead and ascended into heaven. That final transfiguration and glorification of the material universe which the phrase 'the Resurrection of the Body' denotes is indeed a great mystery; we can dimly see what it will involve if we look at the human being in whom it has already happened, our Lord Jesus Christ himself. It does, however, mean that the final glory for which God has made us and to which He calls us will involve every aspect of our being, both mental and physical, and not just our disembodied spirits. And it means in consequence that our life in the Church includes in its embrace our bodies no less than our souls. The notion that religion has as its object the deliverance of our souls from their entanglement with our bodies is a pagan view against which the Christian Church has consistently waged war, though not a few Christians have allowed their religion to be contaminated by it. Not the deliverance of our souls from our bodies, but the sanctification and the supernaturalization of our whole being, body and soul alike—this is the purpose for which the Catholic Church and its whole sacramental equipment exist, and it is for this that the eternal Son of God, the Second Person of the Holy Trinity, took human flesh from a human mother. When this truth is forgotten, the body tends to be looked upon as either inherently evil and antagonistic to the soul and therefore to be ruthlessly mortified and repressed, or else as having no organic relation to the soul and therefore as being outside the concern of religion. Thus we can get either, on the one hand, an attitude of extreme and negative asceticism or, on the other, an attitude of extreme and unbridled sensuality; both of these are equally at variance with the central Catholic doctrine that the body, no less than the soul, is created by God and is made for eternal life with Him.

It is important not to be misled by the use of the word 'flesh' in the Bible, for this is very different from its common use in European languages to-day. It has in fact two meanings in the Bible, which are widely different from each other and are therefore easy to distinguish in their contexts. In some contexts 'flesh' (or 'flesh and blood') simply means human nature in its entirety as created by God and is practically equivalent to our phrase 'body and soul.' When in reply to S. Peter's confession 'Thou art the Christ, the Son of the living God,' our Lord exclaims

'Flesh and blood hath not revealed it unto thee, but my Father which is in heaven,'[2] 'flesh and blood' clearly means simply 'any human agency.' When in S. John's Gospel he asserts 'He that eateth my flesh and drinketh my blood abideth in me and I in him,'[3] what is referred to is the feeding of the whole man upon the whole Christ. When S. John himself tells us that the Word was made flesh,[4] he means that the Word took human nature in its completeness. On the other hand, in other contexts 'flesh' means not just human nature as such but human nature as fallen. Thus, when S. Paul writes that the flesh lusteth against the Spirit and that these are contrary the one to the other,[5] he does not mean that the body lusts against the soul but that fallen man lusts against the Holy Spirit of God. 'Flesh' may thus mean either human nature as such or human nature as fallen; it never, or hardly ever, means the body as contrasted with the soul. The notion that the soul achieves salvation by escaping from the grip of the body is a pagan Greek notion. The teaching of the New Testament is that the whole man, body and soul together, is saved by incorporation into the incarnate Lord who is Himself fully man.

So far is Christianity from an unqualified approval of pure spirituality that it teaches that the spiritual realm, no less than the material realm, has fallen into sin and has rebelled against its Creator. Indeed, in the New Testament evil spirits seem at first sight to be more in evidence than good ones. No doubt this is because the activity of good spirits is so perfectly integrated into the activity of God

[2] Matthew 16: 16–17.   [3] John 6: 56.   [4] John 1: 14.
[5] Galatians 5: 17.

Himself that it does not often need to be distinguished from it. But at least the fact remains that the New Testament has no confidence in spirituality as such. The early Church knew full well, as the Church in many parts of the world knows to-day, that religion can be very spiritual and very evil; this all depends on whom it worships and how it worships him (or her, or it!). The worship which the angels offer to God is purely spiritual, but so is the worship which the devils offer to Beelzebub. Among human religions, devil-worship is about as spiritual as a religion could be. And any one who was tempted to suppose that spirituality as such is good would be well advised to meditate on Dr. C. S. Lewis's *Screwtape Letters.*

Spiritual religion, then, may very well not be Christian, and Christianity is not a purely spiritual religion. Furthermore, spirituality, whether good or bad, need not be religious at all; it may be purely secularist. That is to say, it may be totally uninterested in a transcendent Creator and in any destiny of man beyond his earthly life; it may even deny the existence of either and remain undilutedly spiritual. This would seem to be true, for example, of the outlook of Mr. Aldous Huxley, which, so far from being, as many Christians have supposed, materialistic and sensual, is basically exaggeratedly spiritual; it looks upon all the physical side of man's nature with a kind of fascinated horror, as an outrage upon a spiritual being. But, however much it may exploit some of the emotional accompaniments of religion, it is secularist through and through. As Dr. V. A. Demant has written: 'The essential characteristic of secularism is independent of the nature which secularism gives to what it regards as ultimately real; it is still secularist even when that reality is mental or spiritual, and not only when it is material or biological.' And again: 'The ancient paganisms, the Bible and the Christian Church all have this in common, that they hold the source of all things to be a divine reality which transcends the world as well as operating in it. The secularisms of to-day have this in common, that they hold the meaning of the world to lie within itself.' [6]

There are thus a number of different contrasts which it is vital not to confuse, though in fact they are often confused to the great misfortune of mankind. There is the contrast between the created and the uncreated, there is the contrast between the material and the spiritual, there is the contrast between the natural and the supernatural, and there is the contrast between the evil and the good. According to Christian teaching, God alone is uncreated pure Spirit; creatures may be spiritual, material, or, as in the case of man, mysteriously both; all creatures are good as they come from the hands of God but may have become evil if they have rebelled against Him; and man in the totality of his being, matter and spirit alike, can be raised from his natural level to the supernatural level of union with God.

'The Communion of Saints.' There must, then, be no false spirituality in our religion, but neither must there be any false individualism. There is, of course, a true Christian respect for the individual, and it is savagely menaced by the many forms of collectivist doctrine which are rampant in the world to-day and which look upon the individual

[6] *Religion and the Decline of Capitalism*, pp. 113, 111.

man or woman as having no function or value except as one of the components of a collective, whether this collective be thought of in political or economic or racial or any other terms. In contrast, Christian doctrine affirms that every man and woman has a unique place in God's purpose, that Christ has died for each one as if he or she was the only human being in the universe, and that each one has his or her inalienable responsibility for accepting God or rejecting Him. Neither as the object of God's love nor as the subject of his own responsible acts can any one shelter himself behind the anonymous mass of the collective or submerge his own unique individuality. To each one comes the voice of God saying 'Son of man, stand upon thy feet, and I will speak with thee'[7]; each one can say with S. Paul, 'The Son of God loved me and gave himself for me.'[8] Nevertheless, while in a very real sense every Christian has been saved as an individual, he has been saved into a community. He finds himself not as an isolated individual face to face with his Creator, but as a member of the Body of Christ and the household of God. Indeed the Bible sees the work of Christ as consisting not merely in the gathering of individuals into the Body of Christ, but as the reassembling and reconstituting of the one family and people of God which sin had shattered into fragments. Jesus died, S. John tells us, 'that he might gather together into one the children of God that are scattered abroad.'[9] And in the vision which closes the New Testament, the final condition of affairs when the redemptive work of God in Christ is complete is seen under

[7] Ezekiel 2: 1.
[8] Galatians 2: 20.
[9] John 11: 52.

the image of the new Jerusalem, the holy city which comes down from God out of heaven into which are drawn all the nations of the earth.[10] The life everlasting in the communion of saints through the resurrection of the Body—this is the end for which human beings have been made, and our progress towards it will be vitiated or retarded if we fail to keep it constantly before our eyes.

The first reason, then, why we should consider the beatific vision even while we are still on earth is that it is the goal of our journey. The second reason is that, although its full possession and enjoyment await us in heaven, we are already given a foretaste of it through our membership of Christ in His Body the Church, and therefore that what is true about the life of heaven is also true in its own special way about our life as Christians upon earth. We must, of course, never forget the contrast between the life of grace and the life of glory. Here we are on the journey, *in via*; there we shall be in our fatherland, *in patria*. Now we see in a mirror, darkly; then we shall see face to face. Now we know in part, but then we shall know even as we are known.[11] Now we are the children of God, but it is not yet made manifest what we shall be.[12] Throughout the New Testament the contrast is emphasized between our present and our final condition. Yet at the same time it is made equally clear that the powers of the age to come are already working in us. We are on the journey it is true, but even now our citizenship is in heaven [13]; we know only in part, but nevertheless we know; we see in a mirror, darkly, but nevertheless we see; our future state is not yet manifest, yet

---

[10] Revelation 21.
[11] 1 Corinthians 13: 12.
[12] 1 John 3: 2.
[13] Philippians 3: 20.

we are the children of God. And although we are on the journey and not yet in the fatherland, we are nevertheless no more strangers and sojourners but fellow-citizens with the saints and of the household of God.[14] We have here no abiding city and we seek the city which is to come [15]; yet we have already come to the city of the living God, the heavenly Jerusalem [16] and God has made us to sit with Him in the heavenly places in Christ Jesus.[17] This peculiar dual character of the New-Testament language, which to a superficial glance may appear to be formally self-contradictory, has been too much for the understanding of many Christian people. Some of them, attending to the assertions of the *present* character of our life in Christ, have assumed that the work of Christ was completed in His death and resurrection and that nothing of any religious significance can happen now or will happen in the future; all post-Christian history is just a 'residue,' nothing remains to be done but a little tidying up. Others, concentrating upon the assertions of the *future* consummation, have held that the kingdom of God has not yet been set up and will not be set up until Christ returns in glory; God has forgiven us our sins through the blood of Christ, if we have faith in Him, but we are still as corrupt and pitiful as we ever were. In one respect these views are poles asunder, for one of them holds that everything of significance has already happened, while the other holds that nothing of significance has happened yet. In another respect, however, they agree, namely in holding that nothing of significance is happening now. And they are equally one-sided and over-simplified. What the New Testament is in fact telling us, in

[14] Ephesians 2: 19. [15] Hebrews 13: 14. [16] Hebrews 12: 22.
[17] Ephesians 2: 6.

mysterious images and dark metaphors, is that in our life as members of Christ's Body, we already are given a real but partial participation in those good things of God of which the full enjoyment awaits us in heaven. In the words of a great Christian theologian, 'Grace is nothing else than a kind of beginning of glory in us.' [18] Therefore, everything that is true of the beatific vision will, when all the necessary qualifications have been made to distinguish between our present condition on the journey and our final condition in the fatherland, be true of our life in Christ's Body on earth. To enable us to grasp the essential identity of Grace and Glory is the work of the virtue of Hope, the virtue which enables us to see under the veils of its present imperfect manifestation the glory which will be fully revealed in the future. This paradoxical and double-sided truth, of the reality which is awaited and longed for and yet at the same time already possessed, has received manifold expression in the language of Christian devotion.

> And now we fight the battle,
>   But then shall wear the crown
> Of full and everlasting
>   And passionless renown;
>
> And now we watch and struggle,
>   And now we live in hope,
> And Sion in her anguish
>   With Babylon must cope. . . .
>
> By hope we struggle onward
>   While here we must be fed
> With milk, as tender infants,
>   But there with Living Bread.

[18] S. Thomas Aquinas, *Summa Theologica*, II, II, xxiv, 3.

Yet—

> Jesus! the hope of souls forlorn!
> How good to them for sin that mourn!
> To them that seek thee, O how kind!
> But what art thou to them that find?
>
> No tongue of mortal can express,
> No letters write its blessedness:
> Alone who hath thee in his heart
> Knows, love of Jesus! what thou art.

What, then, can we learn for our life here on earth from S. Augustine's description of the glory of heaven?

11

'We shall rest'

'WE shall rest.' The purpose of activity is rest. It is difficult for us to understand this, in a world in which activity in any form that is not obviously socially harmful has come to be looked upon as self-justifying and in which one of the great archetypal figures of our civilization is that of the big executive, the man who is always in a hurry. There has probably never been a time when there was so much sheer activity as there is to-day, and at the same time when there was so little real co-ordination and unity of purpose. It is not surprising that modern life is riddled with neuroses and frustrations, when there is so much concentration of effort upon minor, though sometimes important, ends and so little conception of any overarching and ultimate purpose of human life.

Mere activity—activity for the sake of activity—is simply diabolical—noise for the sake of noise, bustle for the sake of bustle. It is perhaps significant that, in the Vulgate version of one of the Compline psalms, the devil is described as *negotium perambulans in tenebris,* 'the *business* that prowls around in the shadows,' sheer mischief looking for a loophole by which it can make an entry. 'Damnation,' wrote Miss Dorothy Sayers, that remarkable lay apologist for the Christian religion, 'is without direction or purpose. Why not? It has nothing to do, and all eternity to do it in.'[1]

[1] Dante, *The Divine Comedy. II: Purgatory.* Introduction, p. 61.

George Macdonald described heaven as 'the regions where there is only life and therefore all that is not music is silence,' and in Dr. C. S. Lewis's *Screwtape Letters* the comment of the professional tempter is as follows:

'Music and silence—how I detest them both! How thankful we should be that ever since our Father entered Hell... no square inch of infernal space and no moment of infernal time has been surrendered to either of those abominable forces, but all has been occupied by Noise —Noise, the grand dynamism, the audible expression of all that is exultant, ruthless, and virile—Noise which alone defends us from silly qualms, despairing scruples, and impossible desires.' [2]

It is at this point, in the middle of his frenzied panegyric upon Noise, that Screwtape discovers that he has been transformed into a centipede and has to continue his correspondence with the aid of a secretary.

It is a sinister feature of our civilization that so many of its members not only have little opportunity of genuine interior repose and quiet but are reluctant and unwilling to use it when it comes their way. There is, for example, in the minds of many people a deep fear of the silence of a retreat, and only too often the reason is that in retreat they will be deprived of the constant interruptions and distractions—the *noise*, both literal and metaphorical—which in the conditions of their ordinary life protects them from paying heed to the underlying and disquieting suspicion that the very activity by which their lives are dominated is

[2] *The Screwtape Letters,* no. xxii.

largely pointless and self-frustrating. Noise can in fact make itself louder and louder in order to disguise its own futility.

One consequence of this disordered attitude to activity is that rest itself is misunderstood and perverted. It becomes merely an escape from the exhaustion of continual activity, a mere knocking off from work for the week-end until the hooter sounds again on Monday morning, a rest which takes us *away from* our work. The true pattern of Rest is, however, provided for us in the Book Genesis, where we are told that God blessed the seventh day and hallowed it, because that in it He rested from all His work which He had created and made.[3] There is, of course, a very real sense in which God's activity never ceases at all, since His creative act perpetually upholds and energizes the universe; in our Lord's own words, 'My Father worketh even until now, and I work.'[4] Furthermore, in His own inner being God is not dead or static, but is that unfathomable and inexhaustible energy of life and love which is the Holy Trinity. But all this involves no change in God, no alternation or vacillation of actions. He is the unchanging ground of the changing universe; in the words of the office-hymn for None, He is 'creation's secret force, himself unmoved, all motion's source.' It is His very Rest that maintains a restless universe; in Him Rest and Activity are reconciled. In the language of the scholastic theologians, He is Pure Act, and for this very reason He is unchanging. There is nothing that can be added to Him, for He possesses every perfection already. And nothing can be lost by Him, since pure perfection cannot disintegrate.

[3] Genesis 2: 3.   [4] John 5: 17.

Nevertheless, there is a real truth which is expressed in the anthropomorphic language of the verse in Genesis; it is that God does not, so to speak, turn away in relief from the world which He has made, but contemplates it and rejoices in it. He is not like the wage-slave who tries to forget his work during the week-end break, but rather like a man who makes things as a hobby and gets pleasure from using them when he has made them, or like a painter who can enjoy looking at the picture which he has finished. All such illustrations are, however, inadequate to express the mystery of God's own being; we can only bow our heads in adoration before Him in whom infinite energy is identical with infinite peace, in whom Repose and Power are one.

What is the point of this for us? It is that we are ourselves admitted into this perfect Rest which is God's.

'God saw everything that he had made, and behold, it was very good.'[5] And God made man in His own image, and placed man in the garden which He had made, to dress it and to keep it. And the Lord God spoke with man in the garden in the cool of the day. This paradisaical state of obedience to God and fellowship with Him, for which man was made and in which but for his rebellion he might have grown to a maturity such as we cannot imagine, fed as he would have been by the fruit of the tree of life, what was this but a sharing in God's own rest, the rest in which God rejoiced in the contemplation of the world which He had made and which He saw to be very good? Certainly this would seem to be presupposed by the third chapter of the Epistle to the Hebrews, to which I shall now turn.

[5] Genesis 1 : 31.

The author of the Epistle begins this part of his exposition from a verse in the ninety-fifth psalm, the *Venite,* perhaps the most familiar of all the psalms to those Anglicans who attend Morning Prayer.

'To-day if ye shall hear his voice, harden not your hearts, as in the provocation, like as in the day of temptation in the wilderness.' This was not Adam's sin, but the sin of the Israelites in the Exodus at the places called Meribah and Massah, 'provocation' and 'temptation,' when, in response to their complaints and demands, Moses, against his better judgment, brought forth water from the rock. Nevertheless, the psalmist is explicit that the result of their rebellion, which would seem to be a kind of repetition of the disobedience of Adam, was to exclude them from the Rest towards which they had in fact been journeying, and this rest, the writer tells us, is the rest in which God rested when He had completed the work of creation.

'He [that is, God] hath said: "As I sware in my wrath, They shall not enter into my rest," although the works were finished from the foundation of the world. For he hath said somewhere of the seventh day on this wise, "And God rested on the seventh day from all his works." '

Why, then, did the psalmist, writing long after the Exodus, exhort his hearers to hear God's voice, and not to harden their hearts, 'to-day'? Because, although the Israelites were unable to enter into God's rest, it is still there for us to enter into it. And here a point is made which can easily be missed in the English translation unless we remember that in the Greek in which the Epistle was

written the word which corresponds to the Hebrew name
Joshua is 'Jesus.' 'If Jesus [that is, Joshua the son of Nun,
who led the Israelites into Canaan after the death of Moses]
had given them rest, he [that is, God, or the psalmist
through whose lips He speaks] would not have spoken
afterward of "another day." ' But He did so speak, and so
'there remaineth therefore a sabbath rest for the people of
God.' 'Let us therefore give diligence to enter into that
rest, that no man fall after the example of disobedience.'
The first Jesus, the son of Nun, could only lead the people
of God through the Jordan into Canaan, and, although it
was the land of promise and a land flowing with milk and
honey, what they found there was something that fell very
far short of the sabbath rest of God. But our great high
priest is the second Jesus, the Son of God, who has passed
not just through Jordan but through the heavens [6] and is
now seated on the right hand of the throne of the Majesty
in the heavens [7] and through Him we can draw near to the
throne of Grace and enter into the rest of God.

God's reaction to the sin of man was to re-create through
Christ the world which He had made and which sin had
spoilt. In the Genesis story, the story of the first creation,
it was on the sixth day of the week that God made man in
His image and gave him dominion over the lower creatures:
God 'brought them unto Adam to see what he would call
them, and whatsoever Adam called every living creature,
that was the name thereof.' [8] In the Gospel story, the story
of the new creation, man was re-made by God on the sixth

[6] Hebrews 4: 14.
[7] Hebrews 8: 1.
[8] Genesis 2: 19.

day of the week, the first Good Friday, when Christ, the perfect Man, died on the Cross. And He rested in the tomb on Holy Saturday—the Great Sabbath—in the enjoyment of the work of the new creation. He saw what He had made, and behold it was very good. He looked upon the travail of His soul and was satisfied.

In Judaism itself there was the expectation of the coming great sabbath of the Messianic age, in which God would complete His work and restore the world to its pristine integrity, a time when the blind would receive sight and the deaf would hear, the dumb would speak and the lame would walk, and the dead would be restored to life. And we can hardly doubt that our Lord's miracles are not merely touching works of compassion but are also the signs that the great Sabbath of the Messianic age has arrived. Thus it seems clear that in performing miracles on the sabbath day Christ was not simply flouting the stuffy conventions of His contemporaries and implying that one day was as good as another for the performance of corporal works of mercy. The sabbath is not just a *legitimate* day for the working of miracles; it is the day *par excellence* on which they should be worked, for they are the signs that the Great Sabbath has arrived, the day on which man is admitted once more to the Rest of God. 'Ought not this woman, being a daughter of Abraham, whom Satan had bound, lo, these eighteen years, to have been loosed from this bond on the day of the sabbath?'[9] The consummation of this sabbatical work of re-creation is reached on the sabbath when, having restored human nature to its true relation to God by making in His own tortured body a

[9] Luke 13: 16.

perfect human act of obedience and dedication to the Father in His death on the Cross, the perfect Man lies at rest in the tomb, happy in the fulfilment of His work and awaiting His resurrection. It is thus altogether fitting that the early Church should have chosen Holy Saturday as the normal day for men and women to receive the sacraments of Christian initiation and to be re-created into the Body of Christ.

Thus it is that we have entered into the Rest of God, a rest which is not stagnation, inertia, or boredom, but perfect and unruffled life. God is changeless, not because He is lifeless but because He is fully active and actual, infinite fullness to which nothing can be added and from which nothing can be lost—Trinity of Father, Son and Holy Spirit, united in one perfect circulation and interchange of Love. Our full possession of this rest awaits us in heaven, but its foretaste is given to us here: 'Grace is a beginning of glory in us.' We have already been made 'partakers of the divine nature.' [10] Our life is hid with Christ in God.[11]

Thus, to take but one example of the implications of this truth for our Christian life, in contemplative prayer we are not strictly speaking *passive*, in the ordinary sense of that term, but *receptive*—receptive of God's own self-contemplation, caught up into God's own life and energized by Him. Thus it is that contemplation is the source and the foundation of all truly Christian activity and that many of the great contemplative saints outside their times of prayer, so far from being listless and pallid, have been volcanoes

[10] 2 Peter 1: 4.
[11] Colossians 3: 3.

of activity. But their activity has not been like so much human activity to-day, activity for the sake of activity, unco-ordinated, self-conflicting and self-frustrating; still less has it been mischievous and destructive, like the activity of the 'business that prowls around in the shadows.' It has been unified, coherent and virile, and totally concentrated on one object, the fulfilment of the will of God; for it is in fact God's own energy, drawn by contemplation into the human will, and mastering while at the same time liberating it.

So contemplation is both the end and the source of all truly Christian activity: the end, because our final destiny is to contemplate God in heaven; the source, because Christian activity is simply the overflow of contemplation, proceeding *ex superabundantia contemplationis.*

At this point, however, we have moved into the second stage of our thought: 'We shall rest, and *we shall see.*'

III

'We shall see'

'WE shall rest, and *we shall see*. . . .'

The end of man, we are told, is the vision of God; and our Lord's promise to the pure of heart is that they shall see God.[1] 'As for me,' wrote the Psalmist in a moment of supreme insight, 'I shall behold thy presence in righteousness, and when I awake up after thy likeness, I shall be satisfied with it.'[2] But even he did not know the wonder of the God whom to behold is perfect and inexhaustible beatitude and joy. 'Blessed are the eyes which see the things that ye see,' said our Lord to His disciples, 'for I say unto you, that many prophets and kings have desired to see the things which ye see, and have not seen them; and to hear the things which ye hear, and have not heard them.'[3] And of these things which are revealed to us in Christ none is more wonderful than the fact that God is no simple undifferentiated monad, but is that eternal and infinite ocean of self-giving and self-receiving love, the Ever-blessed and Glorious Trinity.

We can see God; we can know God.

The ancient world knew that for sinful man to look upon

[1] Matthew 5: 8.
[2] Psalm 17: 16.
[3] Luke 10: 23, 24.

God was to die, and many are the myths in which expression is given to the conviction that human sight cannot bear the vision of deity. Thus, to give but one example from classical mythology, when at Semele's request Jupiter, who has wooed her in human form, appears to her in his undisguised splendour, she is struck dead and shrivelled up by his unbearable majesty. And in the Bible itself, when Moses, the great prophet to whom God spoke face to face as a man speaks to his friend and through whom God gave His Law to His chosen people, begged that God would show him His glory, the reply was given: 'Thou canst not see my face; for there shall no man see me and live.' And so God tells him: 'Behold, there is a place by me, and thou shalt stand upon the rock: and it shall come to pass, while my glory passeth by, that I will put thee in a cleft of the rock, and will cover thee with my hand until I have passed by; and I will take away my hand, and thou shalt see my back; but my face shall not be seen.'[4]

There are, it is true, in the Old Testament appearances of God to men, but the note of terror is nearly always present. When Isaiah saw the Lord high and lifted up in the Temple, he cried 'Woe is me, for I am undone . . .; for mine eyes have seen the King, the Lord of hosts.'[5] Although God appeared to Ezekiel by the banks of the Chebar in a form of majesty, it is suggested that His glory was veiled under a symbolic exterior. What Ezekiel saw was 'the *likeness* as the *appearance* of a man.' 'This was the *appearance* of the *likeness* of the *glory* of the Lord.'[6]

[4] Exodus 33.
[5] Isaiah 6: 5.
[6] Ezekiel 1: 26, 28.

And even so, Ezekiel fell on his face with awe at the sight. The Old Testament is clear that the vision of God is insupportable by man. Only very occasionally, as in the Psalm which was quoted at the beginning of this chapter, is there a trace of a further insight. For the world before Christ, to see God was to die.

But we know that, for man restored in Christ, to see God is to live. 'Blessed are the pure in heart, for they shall see God.'

Why is our desire for the beatific vision so weak? Mainly, no doubt, because of our sinful attachment to creatures and the habit which has more and more grown upon us of clutching at the lesser goods which offer us immediate satisfaction, to the neglect of the supreme Good which awaits us in heaven. ' 'Tis ye, 'tis your estrangèd faces, that miss the many-splendoured thing.' But partly, I think, because we have not yet experienced the beatific vision and so have no first-hand knowledge of what it is like. Most of us have at some time had the experience of being persuaded by a friend to make a troublesome journey in order to see some scene of natural beauty or some great work of art. Very probably we have resisted the invitation, because we found it hard to believe that the object was really as entrancing as people made out and that the journey was worth while. And perhaps the matter ended there and we never saw it at all. But on other occasions we yielded to our friend's importunity and went with him. And then we found that the object exceeded in its beauty anything that we could possibly have imagined, and our attitude to our friend changed from a somewhat resentful feeling of grievance to one of delighted gratitude for the insistence with which he had induced us to accompany him.

It is, I suggest, very much like this as regards the beatific vision. We have God's own assurance that it will give us supreme and unfailing joy, and this assurance is endorsed, if indeed it needs endorsement, by the witness of the great mystical saints who have received a transient but genuine anticipation of it in this life. But here we walk by faith and not by sight; we see in a mirror darkly and not face to face. Grace is indeed a beginning of glory, but it is only a beginning. And the faint adumbrations of the vision which we ourselves have experienced are illuminated for us and our confidence in them is immensely strengthened by the witness of those who have in this life been granted what the theologians of mysticism describe as 'an experimental knowledge of God.'

This is all the more important because to us who have been brought up in an industrialized civilization it has apparently become abnormally difficult to recognize God as the creator of the world which surrounds us and which we experience. To the great bulk of mankind throughout its history it has seemed too obvious to need argument that the finite world which impinges upon our senses draws its existence from a reality which lies beyond and behind itself, however dimly and even distortedly the nature of that reality has been conceived. For the Psalmist the fact that 'the heavens declare the glory of God and the firmament showeth his handiwork'[7] is not open to question. Dr. F. Sherwood Taylor has pointed out that 'before the separa-

[7] Psalm 19: 1.

tion of science and the acceptance of it as the sole valid way of apprehending nature, the vision of God in nature seems to have been the normal way of viewing the world, nor could it have been remarked as an exceptional experience,'[8] and Professor Herbert Butterfield has written to much the same effect:

> 'I am not sure that in the modern age, which has produced such a tremendous preoccupation with material things, and has issued in a worldliness hitherto unachieved in our part of the globe, we have not ourselves thickened unnecessarily that screen which amongst the ancient Hebrews was so thin and in some respects so transparent; especially as we, inhabitants of cities, who yet have never really learned how to live in cities, have so greatly lost the art of meditating.'[9]

It may thus very well be the case that for us the knowledge of God which is natural to man, as an inhabitant and a member of a world that God has created, needs help from both the experience of the mystics and from the revelation given through Christ if it is to be adequately evoked and sustained. In any case the fact remains that the contemplation of God's creatures, while it can lead us to set our hearts on them instead of on the God who made them, can, if it is rightly directed, vastly enhance our sense of His reality and His transcendent sovereignty and glory. 'O Lord our Governor,' exclaims the Psalmist, 'how excellent is thy name in all the world, thou that hast set thy glory above the heavens. . . . For I will consider the

[8] *The Fourfold Vision*, p. 91.
[9] *Christianity and History*, p. 117.

heavens, even the works of thy fingers, the moon and the stars which thou hast ordained.'[10] So far from it being necessary for us to despise God's creatures in order for us to give God His due honour, the precise opposite is the case. The more we are conscious of the goodness and the beauty of the finite world, the more fully we shall be brought to recognize the infinite and transcendent goodness and beauty of God, provided only—and this is, of course, essential—that we joyfully recognize Him as their source.

> 'How wonderful creation is, the work which thou didst bless,
> But oh, what then must thou be like, eternal loveliness!
> In wonder lost the highest heavens Mary their Queen may see;
> If Mary is so beautiful, what must her Maker be?'[11]

No Christian writer, to my knowledge, has emphasized the austere aspect of Christian spirituality and the tribulation of spirit to which a Christian may be subjected in his achievement of union with God as has the great sixteenth-century Spanish Carmelite mystic S. John of the Cross. Yet when he attempts to describe the utter beauty and wonder of God he expresses himself in poetic forms which show the most exquisite discernment and appreciation of the beauty and wonder of the natural world:

> 'My love is as the hills
>   The lonely valleys clad with forest-trees,
> The rushing, sounding rills,
>   Strange isles in distant seas,
>   Lover-like whisperings, murmurs of the breeze.

[10] Psalm 8: 1, 3.   [11] Hymn by F. W. Faber.

'My love is hush-of-night,
 Is dawn's first breathings in the heav'n above,
Still music veil'd from sight,
 Calm that can echoes move,
 The feast that brings new strength—the feast of love.' [12]

But most clearly of all in this life, we see God revealed to us in terms that we can understand, in the human nature of the Incarnate Lord, our Saviour Jesus Christ. When Philip came to the Lord with the request 'Lord, show us the Father,' he received the reply: 'Have I been so long time with you, and dost thou not know me, Philip? He that hath seen me hath seen the Father; how sayest thou, Show us the Father? Believest thou not that I am in the Father, and the Father in me? The words that I say unto you I speak not of myself; but the Father abiding in me doeth his works.' [13] For 'God who commanded the light to shine out of darkness hath shined in our hearts to give the light of the knowledge of the glory of God in the face of Jesus Christ.' [14]

We see God in Jesus. We see Jesus in His saints. And in heaven the whole mystical Body of Christ will gaze adoringly upon the face of the Father through the eyes of Jesus, who is its Head.

But now we see through a glass darkly, and not yet face to face. And nowhere perhaps as sharply as in this matter

---

[12] *The Spiritual Canticle,* translated by E. Allison Peers.
[13] John 14: 8–10.
[14] 2 Corinthians 4: 6.

of seeing and knowing God is the contrast drawn between our future heavenly state and our condition as pilgrims on earth.

> 'There dawns no sabbath,—no sabbath is o'er;
> Those sabbath-keepers have one and no more;
> One and unending is that triumph-song
> Which to the angels and us shall belong.
>
> 'Now in the meanwhile, with hearts raised on high,
> We for that country must yearn and must sigh:
> Seeking Jerusalem, dear native land,
> Through our long exile on Babylon's strand.' [15]

It will therefore be useful to consider a little more fully the nature of the virtue of faith, by which we know God on earth and which is so sharply contrasted with the sight which we shall have of God in heaven. Faith, as S. Paul expounds the matter in the First Epistle to the Corinthians,[16] is the first member of the great triad which we know as the theological virtues and whose other two members are hope and charity. It is the first, though not the greatest, for if a man have faith so as to remove mountains and have not charity, he is just nothing. Its great and indispensable feature is that it enables us firmly to hold on to realities which we cannot see. As the Epistle to the Hebrews puts it, 'faith is the giving substance to the things which are hoped for, the discerning of things which are not seen.' [17] It thus has the paradoxical character that it is both very

---

[15] Hymn of Peter Abelard, translated by J. M. Neale.
[16] chapter 13.
[17] Hebrews 11: 1.

obscure and also entirely convincing. S. John of the Cross, who writes about it at length in the Second Book of *The Ascent of Mount Carmel,* insists that faith purifies and perfects the understanding, as hope and charity perform this same service respectively for the memory and the will. It gives us absolute certainty of the reality of God, but it does not do this by making Him visible to us. On the contrary, it is precisely when God cannot be *seen* in any sense of the word that faith does its greatest work for us. It enables us to give substance, to lay hold upon, the things which are *hoped for,* to discern the things that are *not seen.* S. John of the Cross tells us quite explicitly that 'faith, although it brings certainty to the understanding, brings it not clearness but obscurity.'[18] It is just because God exceeds the grasp of our minds that faith is both necessary and fruitful; it is just when we have begun to outgrow the habit of conceiving God in our own image, and in consequence may seem to have lost any power to conceive Him at all, that faith enables us to hold on to Him blindly and to have complete, if agonizing, certainty of the reality of Him whom we cannot see or picture. Thus, for S. John of the Cross faith is specially involved in the dark night of the intellect or understanding, that stage in the spiritual life—and in one form or another it may come to a very ordinary Christian quite early in his religious pilgrimage—when, just because we have begun to rid ourselves of the crude and inadequate ideas of God with which in all probability we began, we may seem to have lost Him altogether. Indeed, one of the regular marks of spiritual progress is the combination of a diminution of the *feeling* of the presence of God with an increase in the

[18] *Ascent of Mount Carmel,* Book II, chapter vi, 2.

conviction of His reality. If this is not understood we may mistakenly suppose that we have gone back in our religion, or even that religion has now shown itself to be a sham, when in fact we have made considerable progress. The explanation is perfectly simple; it is that the more accurately we come to know God, the more fully we understand that His infinite and transcendent being outstrips our finite powers of apprehension. It is precisely in order to enable us to hold on to Him in this situation—to discern the things that we cannot see—that God offers us this paradoxical, but inspiring and invigorating, gift of faith.

And as we gaze in the dark night of faith upon the God whose face we cannot see, if our faith is infused with charity something will happen which others are more likely to observe than we are ourselves; we shall become like that upon which we gaze. This assimilation to God, this becoming like God, so far as it is possible for a creature to become like its Creator, will reach its full expression in heaven after the general resurrection. 'We know,' writes S. John, 'that when he shall appear we shall be like him, for we shall see him as he is.' [19] Nevertheless, the process of assimilation has already begun, and in the previous verse S. John tells us that, although it is not yet manifest what we shall be, nevertheless we are already the children of God. And the same truth is proclaimed by S. Paul even more clearly in the Second Epistle to the Corinthians. 'We all with open face, beholding as in a mirror the glory of the Lord [or should we translate it "reflecting as a mirror the glory of the Lord"?—the result is the same], are transformed into that same image from glory to glory.' [20] From

[19] 1 John 3: 2.   [20] 2 Corinthians 3: 18.

baptism to the beatific vision, from the first movements of grace to its culmination in glory, our adherence to God, in faith which is infused with charity, should make us more and more like that upon which our eyes are fastened. And as the process of assimilation goes on there will come with it a new kind of knowledge of God, a knowledge which is deeper and more intimate than any knowledge which consists merely of looking at something that stands over against ourselves. Its technical name is 'knowledge by connaturality,' and it is the knowledge which one has of something by possessing its character oneself. It is, for example, the knowledge of honesty which a man can have not by being thoroughly acquainted with all the laws, both moral and penal, which are concerned with picking and stealing, but simply by being honest himself. It is the knowledge which, if the illustration may be allowed, we can imagine a conscious and intelligent glove might have of the hand which wore it, simply by *being the same shape* as the hand. M. Jacques Maritain writes about it as follows:

'What is it that makes us radically connatural with God? It is sanctifying grace, whereby we are made *consortes divinae naturae* [partakers of the divine nature]. And what makes this radical connaturality pass into act; what makes it flower into the actuality of operation? Charity. We are made connatural to God through charity. Charity is not just any kind of love. It presupposes sanctifying grace, of which it is the property, and it lays hold of God as He is really present within us as a Gift, a Friend, an eternal life-companion. However, it wins to God immediately as God, in His very deity, in the very intimate and absolutely proper life with which He will beatify us. Charity loves Him in Himself and by Himself.' [21]

And the ultimate reason why, when we gaze upon God in the dark night of a faith which is infused with charity, we are transformed into His likeness is that, although it is true and important that we are looking at God, it is equally true and far more important that He is looking at us. And though our view of Him may indeed be obscure and even distorted, His view of us is entirely clear and penetrates to the depth of our being. 'Now ye have come to know God,' writes S. Paul to his Galatian converts, *'or rather to be known by God.'* [22] So in the Compline psalm we pray 'Lord, lift thou up the light of thy countenance upon us,' [23] and indeed the Vulgate version turns this prayer into a declaration : 'Lord, the light of thy countenance has been stamped upon us.'

However, in speaking about the place of charity in the life of faith, we have already trespassed upon the subject of the next chapter. 'We shall rest and we shall see,' wrote S. Augustine, 'we shall see *and we shall love.*'

---

[21] *The Degrees of Knowledge* (translation of 1959), p. 260.
[22] Galatians 4: 9.
[23] Psalm 4: 7.

IV

'We shall love'

'WE shall rest, and we shall see; we shall see, and *we shall love.*'

'One of the scribes came, and heard them questioning together, and knowing that he had answered them well, asked him, What commandment is the first of all? Jesus answered, The first is, Hear, O Israel, The Lord our God, the Lord is one; and thou shalt love the Lord thy God with all thy heart, and with all thy soul, and with all thy mind, and with all thy strength.'[1]

In view of this explicit utterance of the Incarnate Lord, it is amazing that some modern writers have maintained that the doctrine that we ought to love God is a heresy contrary to the teaching of Holy Scripture. This can, I think, only be explained by the tendency, from which all of us suffer, to distort the facts in order to make them fit in with our already formed prejudices. Certainly the writers in question have been forced to the most desperate straits in order to defend their thesis. Not only have they had to reinterpret S. Augustine, whom persons of their general theological outlook have commonly looked upon as the one really sound Christian teacher between the New Testament and the Reformation, and to make him instead the founder

[1] Mark 12: 28–30.

of medieval Catholicism; they have also had to cry down the teaching of the Johannine writings and regretfully to admit that, as for example in the thirteenth chapter of the First Epistle to the Corinthians, even S. Paul had his lapses. Their most difficult obstacle, however, is provided by the utterance of the Lord Himself which I have just quoted, and in view of this it is difficult not to feel that, in arguing that man's proper attitude to God is not one of love but merely of faith, they have allowed their prejudices to lead them into a head-on collision with Scripture.

Nevertheless, mistaken as they are in denying that man either can love God or ought to try to do so, they are right in asserting that God's own love is primary. On this point S. John and S. Augustine and every Catholic theologian would agree with them, and in fact if we examine the First Epistle of S. John we see that, starting from this agreed position, S. John works out his doctrine of Love in four stages.

First, then *God is Love,*[2] not just loving, but Love—*agapè*—itself. The life of the triune Godhead is a life of perfect love, of perfect and inexhaustible giving and receiving. When we see God, we shall see Love itself.

There is a moving description of the death-bed of one of the early members of the Carmelite reform. It runs as follows:

'Brother Albert of the Virgin, porter of the Convent of the Martyrs, was on the point of death. His coun-

[2] 1 John 4: 8, 16.

tenance was aflame, and shone with a celestial light which rendered it so marvellously beautiful that all were enraptured and silently shed tears of joy. . . . Suddenly Brother Albert cried out in a loud voice: "Oh, I have seen it! Oh, I have seen it! Oh, I have seen it!" and immediately lowering his arms, crossed them on his breast. As he was about to close his eyes, our venerable father John of the Cross hastened to ask him this question: "Brother Albert, what have you just seen?" And he answered, "Love, love" and remained in an ecstasy.'[3]

God, then, in His own self, quite apart from and antecedent to anything that He has done outside Himself, is eternal and self-subsisting Love.

But then, S. John goes on to tell us, 'God first loved us,'[4] that is to say, He loved us before we were able to love either Him or anything else, for it was His love that gave us our very existence. 'Herein is love, not that we loved God, but that he loved us.'[5] We must never forget that God made us, not because there was something lacking to His perfection which we could supply, but because He wished that there should be other beings to share His life and enjoy His love. God created the world 'not to increase His own beatitude nor to acquire it, but in order to manifest His perfection through the good things which by His free choice He bestows on His creatures.' This at least is a doctrine of the Vatican Council upon which all Christians should agree. As S. Thomas Aquinas says, 'God seeks glory

[3] Quoted by J. Maritain in his Introduction to *S. John of the Cross*, by Fr. Bruno, O.C.D., p. xvi.
[4] 1 John 4: 19.
[5] 1 John 4: 10.

not for his sake but for ours.'[6] And, in Père Charles's words, 'The glory of God does not consist in receiving from us something which will make Him richer. It consists rather in giving us the means of being no longer nothing.'[7] The paradoxical consequence follows that, while we owe to God unbounded gratitude and service, since He can claim it by the best of all titles, namely that from Him we have received everything that we have and everything that we are, it is we, and not He, who benefit from our gratitude and service. As Professor H. A. Hodges has written.

> 'He is our King. His claims over us are unlimited and unconditional. He claims every aspect of our being and activity, in every place and at every moment, from the hour of our birth to the utmost reaches of eternity. And in all this He seems not to be making demands on us, but to be satisfying our deepest desires; for He has fashioned us so that only in this complete and unconditional surrender to Him can our own happiness be found.'[8]

As S. Augustine affirmed, in what is perhaps the most frequently quoted sentence from all his writings, it is because God has made us for Himself that our heart can find its rest only in Him.[9]

God's love for us is shown first of all in creation, and this, it must be remembered, does not refer to an isolated act performed in the remote past but to an incessant activity

[6] *Summa Theologica*, II, II, cxxxii, 1.
[7] *Prayer for All Times*, vol. II, p. 60.
[8] *The Way of Integration*, p. 15.
[9] *Confessions*, Book I, chapter i.

of creative love and power by which God sustains us, and the universe of which we are part, at every moment of our existence. It is this unceasing dependence of God's creatures upon Him that makes our natural knowledge of Him possible. To quote from a present-day Cistercian monk: 'There exists some point at which I can meet God in a real and experimental contact with His infinite actuality: and it is the point where my contingent being depends on His love.'[10] And there is a touching and characteristic expression of this fundamental truth in one of the visions of the thirteenth-century English mystic Julian of Norwich:

'He showed me a little thing, the quantity of an hazel-nut, in the palm of my hand; and it was as round as a ball. I looked thereupon with eye of my understanding, and thought: *What may this be?* And it was answered generally thus: *It is all that is made.* I marvelled how it might last, for methought it might suddenly have fallen to nought for little[ness]. And I was answered in my understanding: *It lasteth, and ever shall [last], for that God loveth it.* And so All-thing hath the Being by the love of God.

'In this Little Thing I saw three properties. The first is that God made it, the second is that God loveth it, the third, that God keepeth it.'[11]

Secondly, and even more wonderfully, the love of God is shown in redemption, the making of a new world out of the old. And indeed S. John's mind is so much dominated

---
[10] Thomas Merton, *Seeds of Contemplation*, p. 31.
[11] *Revelations of Divine Love*, edited by Grace Warrack, chapter v.

by the thought of redemption that he takes creation for granted and makes little or no explicit mention of it. 'Herein,' he writes, 'was the love of God manifested in us, that God hath sent his only begotten Son into the world, that we might live through him. Herein is love, not that we loved God, but that he loved us, and sent his Son to be the propitiation for our sins.' [12] And thirdly, the love of God is shown in the innumerable and unpredictable graces which He showers upon us as we go on living the Christian life. 'Of his fullness have we all received, and grace upon grace.' [13]

The third stage in S. John's doctrine of love is concerned with our love for God, and it is a direct consequence of the second. We love God, but only because God first loved us.[14] The fact that God loved us provides us with both the reason for loving God and the power which enables us to do this. For the love which the Christian exercises, whether towards God or towards men, is simply the reflection and the overflow of the love which God has poured into him. So S. Paul writes to the Roman Christians: 'The love of God has been shed abroad in our hearts through the Holy Ghost which was given unto us.' [15] By our union with Christ we are caught up into the love with which the Father and the Son are united in the life of the Holy Trinity, the love which is the Holy Spirit Himself. In His high-priestly prayer the Incarnate Son besought the Father 'that the love wherewith thou lovedst me may be in them, and I in

[12] 1 John 4: 9, 10.
[13] John 1: 16.
[14] 1 John 4: 19.
[15] Romans 5: 5.

them.'[16] 'That you may love God,' says S. Augustine in one of his sermons, 'let him dwell in you *and love Himself through you.*'[17] And the complementary aspect of this truth is expressed by S. John of the Cross, when he says that in the mystical union the soul loves God '*not through itself but through Himself.* . . . It loves through the Holy Spirit, even as the Father and the Son love one another.'[18] 'Thou art the love with which the heart loves thee,' wrote the thirteenth-century Franciscan poet Jacopone of Todi.[19] And we must remember that, although the mystical union is a condition to which very few Christians attain in this life and is moreover a sheer gift of God, it is, in its essence, only the full flowering of the seed which was implanted into every Christian at his baptism. As Mr. E. I. Watkin has written: 'Since mystical experience is an increase and manifestation of sanctifying grace, it does not differ essentially from the hidden life of grace in the souls of all the just.'[20] 'The way from sanctifying grace to beatific glory is one continuous road of increasing supernatural union between the soul and God.'[21]

Closely on the heels of the third stage of S. John's doctrine of love follows the fourth: 'Beloved, if God so loved us, *we also ought to love one another.*'[22] In one place at least he speaks of them together, when he writes, 'We love, because he first loved us,'[23] without specifying the object

[16] John 17: 26.
[17] Sermon cxxviii: 4.
[18] *The Living Flame of Love*, stanza III, 82.
[19] Quoted by M. C. D'Arcy in *The Nature of Belief*, p. 293.
[20] *The Philosophy of Mysticism*, p. 241.
[21] ibid., p. 129.
[22] 1 John iv. 11.
[23] 1 John 4: 19.

of our love. And our Lord Himself, while He clearly distinguishes our duty to love God from our duty to love our neighbour and gives an uncompromising primacy to our love for God, explicitly declares that the two are 'alike': 'The second like unto it is this, Thou shalt love thy neighbour as thyself.'[24] And for S. John the two are so intimately connected that the one is the test of the other: 'If a man say, I love God, and hateth his brother, he is a liar.'[25] The reason which S. John gives for this may at first sight seem surprising: 'He that loveth not his brother whom he hath seen, how can he love God whom he hath not seen?' Surely, we might somewhat ruefully reflect, it is often the fact that we have seen our brother that makes it difficult to love him. It is frequently much easier to feel well disposed towards a distant and anonymous Chinaman or Basuto—for us who do not live in China or Basutoland—than to love the man next door who insists on playing the gramophone with the window wide open or the relation in the same house who always manages to get hold of the newspaper before us in the morning. But it is precisely our readiness to love the brother whom we have seen that shows our love to be genuine and not sentimental, and that therefore tests also the genuineness of our putative love of God. S. Teresa of Avila remarks, with that devastating common-sense which is so characteristic of her that 'we cannot know whether we love God, although there may be strong reasons for thinking so, but there can be no doubt about whether we love our neighbour or no.'[26]

---

[24] Matthew 22: 39.
[25] 1 John 4: 20.
[26] *The Interior Castle,* V, iii, 8.

A great deal has been written in recent years about the difference between the self-regarding love whose Greek name is *eros,* and the self-giving love called *agapè* or 'charity'; and not all that has been written has been helpful. Dr. C. S. Lewis has recently thrown a great deal of light upon the matter in his book *The Four Loves* by distinguishing two further kinds of love, which he calls 'affection' and 'friendship.' I shall not attempt to summarize his elaborate and penetrating discussion, which is easily accessible and needs to be read at length. I shall, however, add a few words about a question which has on at least two occasions in the history of Western Christendom led to fierce controversy, between Peter Abelard and S. Bernard in the twelfth century and between Fénelon and Bossuet in the seventeenth. This is the question whether it is either necessary or possible for us to love God with a completely disinterested love, a love in which we are totally unconcerned with our own welfare and are indeed indifferent to our eternal salvation. At first sight there might seem to be something highly creditable about such an entirely unselfregarding devotion to the God who is supremely worthy of love, but there are two grave objections to it. The first is that the end which God desires above all else for us is that we may achieve complete and permanent beatitude through union with Him, and that it is therefore, to say the least, perverse of us to claim that full-hearted devotion to Him involves indifference to something that He wills. And the second objection is that, since every being that God has made tends naturally to its own perfection, such an attempt is not merely immoral but also pathological. It can lead to such an appalling case as that which is recorded by Mgr. R. A. Knox, of the young priest who, under quietist influence, prayed on his death-bed that God would send him to hell, so that the divine justice and glory might be more fully manifested.[27] The truth surely is that there is nothing sinful in wishing to achieve beatitude, but only in trying to achieve it otherwise than as God has willed. It should surely be a matter for thanksgiving, not for regret, that the one object which can give us full and incorruptible satisfaction is the one object which above all others God has commanded us to seek, namely Himself. For virtue consists not in forced and introverted attempts to purify our motives, but in doing the will of God without too much anxiety as to how pure our motives are. In this way our motives will purify themselves, in the only sense in which they need to be pure. That is to say we shall more and more be willing what God wills, and finding pleasure in doing so. In a superficial sense our love of God may be getting less disinterested rather than more, for the longer we go on doing God's will the more fully we shall find our own fulfilment. There is a story of an old saint, who, when he was asked whether it is easy or hard to love God, replied: 'It is easy to those who do it.'[28] In the end we shall find ourselves willing what God wills and finding happiness in doing so. And this is something for which we should thank God unreservedly. Being happy does not, however, mean being always conscious of one's happiness, any more than having a good digestion means that one is always thinking how well it is working; the contrary is in fact true. In the beatific vision we shall be supremely and immeasurably happy, but we shall not be thinking about our happiness. We shall be thinking about God, and that is why we shall be supremely and immeasurably happy.

[27] *Enthusiasm*, p. 273.
[28] Quoted by C. S. Lewis in *Arthurian Torso*, p. 142.

Regular and careful self-examination is, of course, a most important discipline in the Christian life, but it is possible for us to become so concerned with estimating the precise degree of perfection which we have reached that we allow the end itself to slip out of sight. Too much concern with our own condition may easily lead us into despair on the one hand or presumption on the other, and both of these are sins against the virtue of hope. There is an amusing and instructive cartoon by Mr. Osbert Lancaster of a young monk who, in reply to a rebuke from a senior, is expostulating with outraged conscientiousness, 'But I *am* holier than thou!' And at the other extreme there is the engaging but disquieting figure in Mr. Harry Blamires's novel *Blessing Unbounded* of the sinner who is luxuriating in his sinfulness in the belief that he is being truly penitent. The characters in the story have just been shown films of incidents in their past life, and the narrator takes up his account as follows:

'I saw that one of my predecessors had been overcome like myself. He had withdrawn from his machine and he stood with shaking shoulders, obviously weeping. I went over to him, glad to encounter a fellow-sufferer. He wiped his eyes.

' "You've no idea what I've seen," he said. "I expect it's the worst thing they've ever had to film."

' "I'm ready to dispute that," I said.

' "No, no. Mine's the worst. It's an all-time low. I'm the dregs. You can't imagine."

' "I can," I assured him, "only too well."

' "No, you can't. I'm the scum. I'm a disgrace to my name."

' "What *is* your name?"

' "Smith," he said tragically. "That's my name. It was my father's name too. And I'm not worthy of it."

' "I think you and I feel pretty much the same," I said encouragingly. "I know I'm a worm."

' "Worms crawl," he said. "I'm not fit to crawl."

'There seemed to be no answer to this. Whatever else, Smith was certainly not going to relinquish his claim to pre-eminence in worthlessness.

' "I've broken every commandment," he moaned, "each one more ingeniously than the last. . . .

' "I've committed every sin," he went on, "every sin in the calendar. . . .

' "I'm untouchable. I not only committed every sin; I boasted of it."

' "You're still boasting of it," I said gently, hoping to ease his despair. But it had the opposite effect.

' "I am, I am. That makes it all the worse. I'm still degenerating. I shall go on degenerating."

' "I doubt it," I said. "From what you say, you haven't left much room for further developments in that direction."

' "That's true. I'm as evil as can be already," he groaned, illogically incapable of resisting the claim.' [29]

How much more honest and genuine, because it is so much more concerned with God Himself, is the reply which S. Catherine of Genoa gave to a stupid and self-righteous friar who told her that he was better fitted for loving God than she was, because he was in religion and she was still in the world: 'That you should merit more than myself, is

[29] *Blessing Unbounded*, p. 132f.

a matter that I concede and do not seek, I leave it in your hands. But that I *cannot* love Him as much as you is a thing that you will never by any means be able to make me understand.' 'And she said this with such force and fervour,' her biographer tells us, 'that all her hair came undone, and, falling down, was scattered upon her shoulders!'[30] And Baron von Hügel's comment on the episode is as follows: 'There is probably no scene recorded for us, so completely characteristic of Catherine at her deepest: the breadth and the fullness, the self-oblivion and the dignity, the claimlessness and the spiritual power—all are there.'

It is by becoming progressively more self-forgetful, and not by becoming more self-analytic, that our love of God grows in strength and depth. And perhaps the most effective way of imitating the saints is the indirect way of thanking God for the fact that they have served Him so much better than we. For in the Body of Christ we are not simply concerned with achieving our own individual perfection but with making our own small contribution to the perfection of the whole body. And in its organic union with the holiness of our fellow-members and, above all, with the supreme and spotless holiness of Christ who is the Body's Head, our own feeble essays in holiness are clothed with a glory and stamped with a value of which in isolation they would be utterly incapable. In this sense at least, the doctrine of the treasury of merits expresses a profound truth.

There is a beautiful Latin hymn by S. Peter Damien

[30] Quoted by F. von Hügel, *The Mystical Element of Religion*, vol. I, p. 141.

about the joys of heaven which expresses this truth of the mystery of coinherence better than anything else which I know, though it loses its concision sadly in translation. In the heavenly country, he tells us, 'although every one's merit differs according to the work which he has done, nevertheless love acquires as its own possession that which it loves to have found in someone else. And so the private property of each becomes the common property of all.'[31]

And Thomas Merton tells us that 'the saints are glad to be saints, not because their sanctity makes them admirable to others, but *because the gift of sainthood makes it possible for them to admire everybody else.*'[32]

In S. Bernard's exquisite little treatise upon the love of God, the progress of the human creature in the life of love is divided into four stages or degrees. First there is the love of man for himself, and S. Bernard is thoroughly realistic in recognizing that this is where we have to start. 'First that which is natural and then that which is spiritual,' he quotes from S. Paul, and 'Who ever hated his own flesh?' And this, in virtue simply of our common humanity, will issue in love of our neighbour, though this will be badly disordered unless God is at its root. And as soon as the man begins to understand his need of God for the satisfactory conduct of his life, he will then begin to love God, though he will be loving God not for God's sake but for his own;

---

[31] *Licet cuique sit diversum pro labore meritum,*
  Caritas hoc facit suum quod amat in altero.
  Proprium sic singulorum fit commune omnium.
The hymn, which begins *Ad perennis vitae fontem,* is printed in J. S. Phillimore's *Hundred Best Latin Hymns,* p. 45.
[32] *Seeds of Contemplation,* p. 43.

this is the second degree of love. The third degree comes when the man sees that God is supremely lovable, not for the gifts that He bestows but for what He is in Himself; and when this conviction becomes dominant, God is being loved for God's own sake and not only for man's. The fourth degree, S. Bernard tells us, cannot be perfectly fulfilled in this life; in it the body—and it is significant that S. Bernard says 'the body' and not just 'the soul'; he is thinking of the full reintegration of man in the general resurrection—will love even itself only for the sake of God.[33]

This rather stylized scheme—self for self, God for self, God for God, self for God—may appear somewhat artificial, but the truth which it contains is profound. There is none of the violent opposition of *eros* to *agapè,* which has made the discussions of some recent writers unrealistic and inhuman. The early stages are not looked upon as bad in themselves but merely as imperfect, even the love of self for self. Each is integrated into the next and so receives its fulfilment. Then—and this is particularly welcome in a medieval writer—there is the most explicit emphasis upon the part which the body has to play in man's final beatitude. S. Bernard indeed writes: 'I think myself that the command to love the Lord our God with all our heart and soul and strength will not be perfectly fulfilled until the mind no longer needs to think about the flesh, and the soul ceases having to maintain the body's life and powers.' But he immediately adds:

> 'In the spiritual and immortal body, the body perfected, at peace and unified, the body made in all things

[33] See *Saint Bernard On the Love of God,* translated by a religious of C.S.M.V., chapters viii–xi.

subject to the spirit, there [the soul] may hope to reach the fourth degree of love—or, rather, to be taken into it, for it is not attained by human effort but given by the power of God to whom he will.

'No wonder if the body glorified thus confers glory on the soul, since even in its weak and natural state it did it no small service. How truly did he speak who said, "All things work together for good to them that love God!" The body serves the spirit in its weakness first, then in its death, and lastly in its resurrection. In the first state it bears the fruit of penitence; in death it gives the spirit rest; and at the last it brings her to that final bliss which rightly she would not desire without its company, since she knows well that in her every state it has served her for good.

'Clearly a good and faithful comrade is the body to a soul well disposed.'

S. Bernard even goes so far as to see the absence of the body between death and resurrection as constituting a definite obstacle to the soul's attempt to love God perfectly:

'The soul has not yet come to self-forgetfulness while yet she looks to get her body back. But when she *has* received it, and that, her only lack, has been supplied, what lets [that is, hinders] her now from going forth from self, as you might say, and passing over into God entire, becoming thus wholly unlike herself in that it now is given her to be supremely like to God?...

'Before death, while still in mortal bodies, we eat the labours of our hands laboriously. But after death we drink, as disembodied spirits, and with a certain most delightful ease we quaff what we receive. And at the last, our bodies given back in deathless life, we are inebriated by love's draught, rejoicing in its marvellous plenitude. . . .

'Now from henceforth do we possess for ever that fourth degree of love, when God is loved supremely and alone; for we no longer love ourselves save for His sake, and He Himself becomes His lovers' recompense, reward eternal of eternal love.'[34]

There has been much false spirituality in medieval and still more in modern religious writing, but clearly there is none of this in S. Bernard's treatise on the Love of God. If if has a defect, it is in a certain neglect of the *social* nature of our final beatitude—of the fact that the resurrection of the body is also the resurrection of Christ's Mystical Body, that we shall be caught up to God in the communion of saints as members of Christ.

M. Jean-Paul Sartre is not a writer to whom one would normally turn for Christian instruction; nevertheless from his play *Huis Clos* ('Secret Session') there is, I believe, a profound religious lesson to be learnt. In this play, three characters, two women and a man, find themselves together after death. All of them have died by violent or ambiguous means, under circumstances that are *prima facie* disgraceful. Each of them is interested in the others as an

[34] ibid., pp. 67, 68, 71, 74, 76.

audience for his or her own attempts at self-justification and displays of self-pity. None of them is interested in the others from any other point of view. None of them shows any sign of either gratitude or penitence; all are resentful and bitter. Each, in short, is interested simply in himself or herself. As the play proceeds, it becomes plain that these three persons are doomed to remain alone together throughout eternity. The unheeded arguments repeat themselves in endless circles and the emotional tension becomes unbearable. As the curtain descends on the scene of never-ending and ever-mounting frustration, its significance is summed up in two desperate exclamations: *Nous serons ensemble pour toujours! L'enfer, c'est les autres!* 'We shall be together for ever! Hell is other people!'

The significant fact is that on other lips these sentiments might be descriptions of the joys of heaven. 'We shall be together for ever'—the communion of saints in the life everlasting. 'Heaven is other people'—'love acquires as its own possession that which it loves to have found in someone else, and so the private property of each becomes the common property of all.'

For, in heaven, S. Augustine tells us, thinking of the union of Christ's members with their head, 'there shall be one Christ, loving Himself.'[35] This is the consummation of love.

---

[35] *On the Epistle of John, to the Parthi,* 10: 3.

V

'We shall praise'

'WE shall rest, and we shall see; we shall see, and we shall love; we shall love, and *we shall praise.*'

In the middle ages there was a vigorous controversy between the theologians of the Dominican and the Franciscan schools on the question whether our beatitude in heaven will consist primarily in the knowledge of God or the love of God, in *seeing* Him or in *loving* Him. The Dominicans, following their great teacher S. Thomas Aquinas, identified the primary constituent of beatitude with the knowledge of God; they could appeal for support to the Lord's own promise that the pure in heart are blessed since they shall see God, and the very phrase 'Beatific *Vision,*' which has become the accepted technical term to designate the heavenly condition, shows how preponderant the Thomist view has been. (It must be remembered that, for Thomists, sight is the most exalted of the five senses and therefore provides the least inadequate image of a purely intellectual activity.) On the other side, the Franciscans, following S. Bonaventure, taught that it is the love of God in which beatitude primarily consists, and they could with some show of cogency invoke the weighty authority of S. Augustine; we may remember that Professor Burnaby's great study of S. Augustine's spirituality bears the title *Amor Dei,* 'The Love of God.' Neither side, of course, denied that beatitude includes both knowledge and love; the question was which of the two was primary. The Thomist argument was that you cannot love what you do not know and that, therefore, in the life of heaven the knowledge which the blessed have of God must be logically and metaphysically prior to the love with which they love Him; but they never asserted that you can come to the full knowledge of God in heaven unless you have loved Him first on earth. The Franciscans, on the other hand, were mission preachers by vocation, and philosophers only, as it were, by accident. They naturally appealed to the emotions rather than to the mind, and when they did appeal to the mind it was to the will rather than to the intellect; this emphasis led them as a matter of course to see beatitude as consisting in the love, rather than in the knowledge, of God.

It is possible that the importance of the controversy has been somewhat exaggerated. As G. K. Chesterton remarked, 'Whether the supreme ecstasy is more affectional than intellectual is no very deadly matter of quarrel among men who believe it is both, but do not profess even to imagine the actual experience of either.'[1] It may be sufficient to echo the words of that remarkable twelfth-century mystic and theologian Hugh of S. Victor, writing before the dispute had got under way:

'In two ways God dwells in the human heart, to wit, through knowledge and through love; yet the dwelling is one, since every who knows Him loves, and no one can love without knowing. Knowledge, through cognition of

[1] *S. Thomas Aquinas*, p. 111.

the Faith, erects the structure; love, through virtue, paints the edifice with colour.'[2]

Both the Thomist and the Franciscan view get into difficulties over the question of disinterestedness. It has often been urged against the Thomist that, if beatitude consists primarily in knowing God, it is really fundamentally selfish. Heaven will consist in enjoying ourselves, even if we are enjoying ourselves in enjoying God. For to know something is to possess it for your own contemplation, to feed upon it intellectually, to clasp it to yourself, to draw it into your mind; it is to make the object your *own*. Love, in contrast we are told, is essentially outgoing and disinterested; only if beatitude consists primarily in *loving* God can it be free from all taint of egoism.

At this point, however, another chorus of voices raises its protest. As I remarked in the last chapter, at least twice in the history of Western Christendom the very possibility of disinterested love has been called in question. In the twelfth century, in the famous dispute between Abelard and S. Bernard, the latter, with that sturdy realism which so often characterizes the saints, insisted that, since our love for God does in fact make us eternally happy and since we know that it does, to demand that we shall love God without regard for our eternal happiness is to demand a psychological impossibility. Even in heaven we are bound to love ourselves, even if paradoxically we can be described as loving ourselves for the sake of God. Furthermore, since it is God's will that we shall be eternally happy, to be

[2] The Moral Ark of Noah, I, ii; quoted by H. O. Taylor, *The Medieval Mind*, vol. ii, p. 397.

indifferent to our eternal happiness would be to be indifferent to the fulfilment of God's will. And to be indifferent to the fulfilment of God's will would be an odd way of manifesting our love for God. Abelard, however, with the uncompromising ruthlessness of the penitent sinner, would have no such truckling with the lust of the flesh, even in a sublimated form; unless I love God without consideration of my own happiness, I am not loving God at all, but only myself.

M. Étienne Gilson has made the penetrating suggestion that Abelard's position is the direct outcome of his tragic affair with Heloise. Abelard, he points out, was full of remorse for the ruin which his passion had brought upon the unhappy partner of his sin, though it might well appear that he had suffered for it more than she had. Heloise herself, with a noticeably feminine tendency to dramatize the situation, was never tired of insisting that both her initial lapse and her subsequent renunciation were entirely the result of her concern for Abelard's happiness, and Abelard, with masculine simplicity, was only too ready to believe her. What, then, does his doctrine of the disinterested love of God come to in the end? Simply this, that a man must love God not as Abelard loved Heloise, but as Heloise loved Abelard. No wonder this was more than S. Bernard could stomach![3]

The second resurgence of the controversy was in the seventeenth century between Bossuet and Fénelon. Here it was the saintly Fénelon who was the champion of disinterested love, and the rather more worldly Bossuet who

[3] É. Gilson, *The Mystical Theology of S. Bernard*, Appendix II.

opposed him. But it would be generally admitted that, if the saintly Fénelon had a fault, it was a rather fastidious pretiosity.

But it is at this point that the windows are thrown open by the Protestants, who let in the icy blast of Lutheranism. What, they demand, is this nonsense about man loving God with a purely disinterested love? Not only is such a love a psychological impossibility, but even if it were possible it would be valueless. The only disinterested love is God's love for man; that is the only *agapè* there is. Any love that man can have for God is sheer *eros,* and to say that a man ought to exercise *agapè* towards God—this is simply to introduce justification by works in its most insidious form. God has love towards man, yes. And let man have *faith* towards God—that will justify him. But that man should have love towards God—this is nothing but the rankest Catholicism. You will not find it in S. Paul, says Dr. Anders Nygren in his great work *Agapè and Eros,* and if S. John was unfortunately under its influence and so infected Christendom with a heresy with which even the great Augustine, that former hero of Protestants, was deeply tainted, the true Pauline doctrine emerged again with Luther. So let us hear no more about man loving God. Did Luther write two million words for nothing?

I have tried to show in the last chapter that a man is neither able nor required to love God with a love that is disinterested in the drastic sense demanded by Abelard and Fénelon, but that nevertheless the kind of love which he can exercise can lead him to a deeper and deeper union with God which will culminate in the beatific vision, since he is being drawn ever more and more intimately into the love which is God Himself. I think that these unhappy controversies at least make one thing plain, that the question of our ultimate attitude to God cannot be solved simply by consideration of knowledge and love, and it is surely most significant that, in the sentence which I have taken as the basis for this book, S. Augustine passes on from both knowledge and love to praise. 'We shall rest and we shall see, we shall see and we shall love, we shall love and *we shall praise*.'

Now praise has a highly paradoxical character, especially the praise of God. The sole justification for praising God is that God is praiseworthy. We do not praise God because it does us good, though no doubt it does. Nor do we praise Him because it does Him good, for in fact it does not. Praise is thus strictly *ecstatic,* in the sense that it takes us wholly out of ourselves; it is purely and solely directed upon God. People have often tried to attribute this ecstatic character to love. They are right in demanding that our primary attitude to God should be disinterested, but wrong in attributing this characteristic to love. So long as we are merely *loving* God, the inherent duality of love is inescapable. We cannot separate loving God for His sake from loving Him for our own sake, even when we can distinguish these two elements in our love. And in so far as we do succeed in loving God for His sake we are in danger of falling into the snare of supposing that we are conferring some benefit upon God, and that is an impossibility. We had far better frankly admit that when we love God we are—and are meant to be—loving Him for our sake. It is altogether different with praise. Praise is entirely directed upon God. It takes our attention entirely off ourself and concentrates it entirely upon Him. It neither does God any good, nor does it profess to do so. Its sole and sufficient justification lies in the fact that God is praiseworthy. And that is all the justification that it needs.

I would add that the way in which we can most effectively purge our love of God from self-centredness is not by essaying the impossible task of achieving a purely disinterested love, but by infusing our love with praise.

In case this conclusion seems too paradoxical to be accepted, I will reinforce it with an illustration from ordinary life. When we are caught up in admiration of a great work of art or a beautiful natural object, what is our justification for being thus occupied? Not that the contemplation of it does us good, though it may well do so. And not that it does the object of our contemplation any good, for it does not. I do not say 'What a lot of good it is doing me to admire that picture!' It is only rather second-rate works of art that produce that reaction. What I say is 'What a splendid picture that is!' And that is sufficient. The same is surely true about a noble human action. It may improve my character to admire it, but that is not what I admire it for. I admire it because it is admirable. In practice, of course, we can only approximate to this state of affairs, and this for two reasons. First, because few, if any, finite beings are *entirely* admirable; there are nearly always some flaws in their perfection which evoke a critical note in our reaction to them. And, secondly, because in this life we seldom or never admire without doing something more. We go in order to admire but to do something else as well. But with these qualifications the illustration may hold. We admire things simply because they are admirable, and the question 'What good does admiring them do?,' while it is interesting and can be important, is fundamentally irrelevant.

I am not denying that it is right to love either finite beings or God, but only that loving them can ever be entirely disinterested. I am, on the other hand, asserting that praise can be. And it is not irrelevant to observe that, even on the human level, love at its highest is always caught up into praise. This is what transfigures all great Christian love-poetry, as, for example, that of Dante or, in our own day, of Gilbert Keith Chesterton. And it is singularly lacking in the *Vivamus, mea Lesbia, atque amemus* of the pagan Catullus.

Praise, then, I suggest has primacy over both knowledge and love, though it may include and transfigure them both. For praise is indifferent to utility and is solely concerned with glory. It is an inspiring thought that in heaven our total concern will be with something that is entirely right and is of no use. In the beatific vision all our human utilitarian economic standards are irrelevant. 'In heaven,' writes the economist Mr. D. L. Munby, 'no problem of scarcity arises, and in hell no possibility of choice exists; economics is a science dealing with the conditions of human life in this world.'[4] Our whole business, says S. Augustine, will be the praise of God. 'All our activity will be Amen and Alleluia,' the Amen which gladly assents to all that God is and all that He has done, and the Alleluia which praises Him for it.

[4] *Christianity and Economic Problems,* p. 44.

'Because our vision of the True will be without satiety, in perpetual delight, because our contemplation will have the perfect assurance of immediacy—kindled, then, by the love of Very Truth, cleaving to Him in the pure embrace of spirit, our spirit's voice will praise Him and say Alleluia. Uplifting one another to the same praise, in most fervent love to one another and to God, all the citizens of that city will say Alleluia,. inasmuch as they will say Amen.' [5]

Conscious perhaps of some marked falling off in the fervour of the faithful in his cathedral city of Hippo as Eastertide wore on, the great bishop and teacher takes pains to emphasize that we shall never weary of our heavenly occupation:

'When we see Him as He is, we shall be like Him; and being like Him, how should we fail, by what should be distracted? Let us rest assured, my brethren. We shall not be wearied by the praise of God, nor by His love. If your love should fail, so would your praise; but if love will be everlasting, because the beauty of God will be uncloying, inexhaustible, fear not that you will lack power ever to praise Him, whom you will have power ever to love.' [6]

And this will be no isolated individual act, but the coherent offering of the risen Body of Christ: 'The peace of the heavenly city is the perfectly ordered, perfectly united fellowship *in the enjoyment of God and of one another in God.*' [7]

[5] Sermon ccclxii, 29.
[6] Enarration on Psalm 83: 8.
[7] *The City of God,* Book xix, chapter 13.

Now, as we have constantly reminded ourselves, grace is a beginning of glory in us, and so all that has been said above is relevant to our present condition. To quote from S. Augustine yet again:

> 'When we see Him face to face, nothing can be better than to be joined fast to Him. But *now*, here in my pilgrimage, when the fulfilment is not yet, what is my good? *To set my hope in God.* So long as you are not yet fast joined to Him, set there your hope. . . . Cleave to Him in hope. And here, setting your hope in God, what will you have to do? *That I may announce all thy praises in the courts of the daughter of Sion.* What will be your work, but to praise Him you love, and to make others share your love of Him?' [8]

To offer praise to God, then, is the primary activity and function of the Christian Church. 'Through him,' we are exhorted in the Epistle to the Hebrews, 'let us continually offer up a sacrifice of praise to God, that is, the fruit of lips which acknowledge his name.' [9] As the words 'through him' (that is, through Christ) show, this sacrifice of praise is something far greater than the mere uttering of praises by individual Christians. The very phrase 'sacrifice of praise' is the name given in the Greek version of the Old Testament—the version which was most familiar to the New Testament writers—to the peace-offering, the one form of sacrifice which it was believed would continue when the Messiah came into His kingdom. In the Hebrew

---

[8] Enarration on Psalm 72: 34. See the admirable exposition in J. Burnaby, *Amor Dei*, chapter viii, 4, from which the above quotations are taken.
[9] Hebrews 13: 15.

text it is called 'the sacrifice of thanksgiving.' The praise which the Church offers to God, then, is the praise which is offered by Christ Himself, a praise which in its primordial essence is the filial response made by the Son to the Father in the life of the Blessed Trinity, finding its expression in human nature when the Son became man in His Incarnation, and taking us up into itself through our incorporation into the incarnate Son in our baptism.

Thus, when in the English Prayer Book the Eucharist is described as 'this our sacrifice of praise and thanksgiving,' what is to be understood by this phrase is the offering of Himself which the eternal Son perpetually makes to the praise of the eternal Father and which has become *ours* because we have been made members of *Him*. The praise which the Church offers in its Offices and its non-liturgical services, and the praise which Christians offer in what we misleadingly call their 'private prayers,' are simply an extension of this. And through his participation in the Church and in the Eucharist the whole life of the Christian —his work and his play, no less than his prayer and his communion, are gathered into the unceasing offering of praise which the ascended Lord ever presents to the glory of His Father in heaven.

'There we shall rest and we shall see; we shall see and we shall love; we shall love and we shall praise. Behold what shall be in the end and shall not end.' But here and now we announce God's praises in the courts of the Daughter of Sion.

VI

The Things that are not Shaken

WE have been considering in this book four aspects of the Beatific Vision which, since grace is a beginning of glory in us, are also experienced by us, although partially and inchoately, in our life as members of Christ in the Church Militant upon earth. I think it will be useful to bring the book to a close by saying something about the notes of Christian living which mark off the Church from the secularized community which surrounds it and which it is sent by Christ to redeem.

In the earliest days of the Church's life the difference between Christians and other people was too conspicuous to be ignored. Christians were clearly living a different kind of life; not just a *better* one, but a *different* one. They were people to whom something very odd had happened. It was not that they never did anything wrong; far from it. They had their failings, and these were sometimes very serious. How serious they could be we can see from the first chapter of the Epistle of S. Paul to the Corinthians. And yet the Church was so obviously filled with love and joy and peace that it was impossible to blind oneself to the fact. You might find yourself being drawn by this; you might, on the other hand, find yourself being repelled by the demands that you felt it was making for your allegiance. But once you had been brought into contact with it you could never quite forget it.

Christians themselves described what had happened to them in what were to the outsider very strange ways. It was all connected with a young man named Joshua or Jesus, who had been executed for sedition in Palestine, a country which was as turbulent in that century as it had been in this, and who, according to them, although he had quite certainly died and been buried, had come back to life again and had been taken up into heaven. They said that they themselves, when they became members of the society which he had founded, had died with him and had risen with him from the grave, and that they had become actual parts of his resuscitated body; and, although it was perfectly plain, both to them and to every one else, that they were still on this earth, they said that they were sitting with him at God's right hand in heaven. They also said that, when they met together each week to celebrate his return to life, he fed them with his own body and blood. All this was very puzzling and difficult to understand. But the fact remained that these people were different; something very remarkable had happened to them, however unintelligible was the description which they gave of it. The Church was a society in which men and women were living with a new kind of life. And so people found themselves forced to decide what their attitude to this new thing was to be. They had either to love it or to hate it; to give themselves to it, or to thrust it away from them.

Now, all this is much more difficult to see to-day, after nineteen centuries of Christianity, when, at any rate in most countries, to say that one is a Christian may mean little more than that one refrains from blasphemy and the more spectacular forms of vice and keeps oneself out of the hands of the police. And it must be admitted that the three characteristic notes of this new life will not be found notably evident in those whose profession of Christianity is cynical, conventional, tepid or merely nominal. But they are in some measure experienced by any one who, however imperfectly and with however many failures, is trying seriously, conscientiously and above all humbly, to live as a follower of Jesus Christ in the fellowship of His Church. And they are incandescently manifest in those who have consistently and unreservedly given themselves to God in Christ, those whom the Church proudly commemorates under the title of Saints.

The first of these notes can be summed up in the word *intensity*. 'I am come,' Jesus Himself declared, 'that they might have life and have it more abundantly.'[1] The great Christian saints are not anæmic or invertebrate specimens; nor are they all of one uniform type, in spite of the way in which religious art, one can only suppose under the inspiration of the devil, has so often depicted them. They are men and women living with tremendous zest and concentration and, because of this, manifesting the most baffling and kaleidoscopic variety of character and activity, since God has taken hold of their individual personalities and developed them to the full. There is literally nothing that is common to them except the intensity of the love which they bear towards God, a love which, as they themselves insist, is not something that they have manufactured

[1] John 10: 10.

for themselves but is nothing less than God's own love, which He has communicated to them. And, like other people in love, they are sometimes led to do things which to others—and sometimes even to themselves—appear imprudent, hazardous and even downright ridiculous. But, as we have already seen, however active they are, the heart of their life is not action but contemplation, the contemplation of God Himself in His infinite energy, love and power; and it is from this contemplation that their activity is derived. And so the activity of the saints is not, like the activity of so many people at the present day, sporadic and unco-ordinated, but is altogether coherent and is concentrated into an irresistible stream of power, since it is nothing less than God's own power flowing out into the world through the consecrated lives of His servants.

First, then, the intensity of Christian living, and now, secondly, the *vastness* of the world in which the Christian lives and of the perspective in which he see things.

The Christian's horizon is not limited by the short span of seventy years or so that lie between the cradle and the grave, nor are the good things to which he can look forward confined to the prizes of wealth, comfort, power and fame which offer themselves to his ambition, or even to those higher goods of science, art or human friendship which one earthly life can contain. How terribly constricted is the world of the secularized man, constricted in space, in time and in human population!

For the Christian, however, life stretches out beyond the grave into an eternity of unimaginable amplitude and richness; and the society to which the Christian belongs is not just of the handful of people whom he can meet on earth and from whom he must part almost as soon as he has met them, but embraces in its scope all God's servants from the world's creation to its final dissolution and all the angelic hosts of heaven. 'Mine,' wrote S. John of the Cross exultantly,

> 'are the heavens and mine is the earth; mine are the people, the righteous are mine and mine are the sinners; the angels are mine and the Mother of God, and all things are mine; and God Himself is mine and for me, for Christ is mine and all for me. What, then, dost thou ask for and seek, my soul? Thine is all this, and it is all for thee.' [2]

Those quaint old-fashioned names which we find in the Calendar—Polycarp, Tryphena and the rest—are not there because the Church is incurably antiquarian, living perpetually in the past, a kind of religious Society for the Preservation of Ancient Monuments, herself the most ancient of all, but because these men and women to whose courage and devotion the Church owes so much are alive to-day; because in Christ they are not our predecessors but our contemporaries.

> 'Ye are come unto mount Sion and unto the city of the living God, the heavenly Jerusalem, and to an innumerable company of angels, to the general assembly and church of the firstborn, which are written in heaven,

[2] *Spiritual Sentences and Maxims*, 25. (*Works*, translated by E. Allison Peers, vol. III, p. 244.)

and to God the judge of all, and to the spirits of just men made perfect, and to Jesus the mediator of the New Covenant.'[3]

And in this vast and splendid world in which the Christian lives, it is God Himself who is the Christian's beatitude. 'If any man love me,' declared the Lord, 'my Father will love him, and we will come unto him and make our abode with him.'[4]

And when we see God face to face we shall find again in Him, in a far more wonderful way, anything that we have had to give up for His sake, and everything good that we have left behind on earth. For in the last resort there are only two alternatives: either to have God, and in Him everything, or to have nothing but yourself. The latter alternative is what Christian theology knows as hell, the former as heaven.

Intensity, vastness, and finally the note of *permanence*.

The most tragic strain in human existence lies in the fact that the pleasure which we find in the things of this life, however good that pleasure may be in itself, is always taken away from us. The things for which men strive hardly ever turn out to be as satisfying as they expected, and in the rare cases in which they do, sooner or later they are snatched away. That is why so many who start out with high hopes and buoyant hearts to enjoy life to the full end up as disgruntled and cynical old men.

[3] Hebrews 12: 22–4.
[4] John 14: 23.

One of the most haunting features of the world's literature—and especially of the literature of the ancient pagan world—is the recurrent sense of the transience and elusiveness, the fragility and fleetingness of even the best things that life can offer, the note of heartbreak at the very root of things. Swinburne's 'Thou hast conquered, O pale Galilean; the world has grown grey from thy breath' embodies a grotesque falsehood. The pagan world was a world which felt the clutch of death at its heart, a world whose very joy was at the best only a brave attempt to prevent the mind from dwelling on the ultimate frustration and destruction of all man's noblest hopes. 'Human life in the ancient world,' wrote Bernard Manning, was 'at its best a comic tragedy played in a picturesque and dignified cemetery.'[5] We may remember that Catullus, in the very poem in which he repudiates the morality of the grave and censorious and calls his Lesbia to throw herself into his arms to enjoy what he alleges to be the summit of human bliss, voices this ultimate despair. What is his reason for it all? Simply this, that we must take all we can while we can, for it will all be snatched away from us when we die.

> 'When the sun sets, it sets to rise again,
> But for us, when our brief day is over,
> There is one endless night that we must sleep.'

Nox est perpetua una dormienda—perhaps the most shattering line that has ever been written.

We turn from this to S. Augustine. In him we find the same sense of the transitoriness of earthly things, but in

---

[5] *Essays in Orthodox Dissent*, p. 68.

him it is combined with the assurance of the things that do not pass away. In his writings the world's heartbreak is expressed with no less poignancy, but with this there is confidence and peace, in the assurance that, when the things that are shaken are removed, the things which cannot be shaken will remain. 'All this most lovely fabric of things that are truly good, when its course has been fulfilled, will pass away; for they have their morning and their evening.'[6] But, in the words which I have taken as the text of this book, 'we shall rest, and we shall see; we shall see, and we shall love; we shall love and we shall praise. Behold what shall be in the end and shall not end.'

For the Christian, all those partial, broken and fleeting perfections which he glimpses in the world around him, which wither in his grasp and are snatched from him even while they wither, are found again, perfect, complete and lasting in the absolute beauty of God, with whom is no variableness, neither shadow of turning.

Intensity, vastness, permanence—utter satisfaction; these are the notes of the life to which God invites us. In their fullness they await us in the life to come, if we have served God faithfully on earth. But even while we are on earth we can experience them in part, if our ultimate loyalty is not to the world but to God, and if we are ready humbly, perseveringly and hopefully to live the life of prayer and sacrament in the Body of Christ.

What is our attitude to this world to be? Treat it as if it is all that there is and as if all that you need is to be

[6] *Confessions,* Book XIII, chapter xxxv.

found in it, and it will dangle its gifts before your eyes, decoy you, tantalize you, and finally mock and desert you, leaving you empty handed and with ashes in your mouth. But treat it as the creation of God, as truly good because it is God's handiwork and yet not the highest good because it is not God Himself, live in this world as one who knows that the world is God's and yet as one who knows that his true home is not here but in eternity, and the world itself will yield up to you joys and splendours of whose very existence the mere worldling is utterly ignorant. Then you will see the world's transience and fragility, its finitude and its powerlessness to satisfy, not as signs that life is a bad joke with man as the helpless victim, but as pale and splintered reflections of the splendour and beauty of the eternal God—that beauty ever old and ever new [7]—in whom alone man can find lasting peace and joy.

'All our activity will be Amen and Alleluia.' 'There we shall rest, and we shall see; we shall see, and we shall love; we shall love, and we shall praise. Behold what shall be in the end, and shall not end.'

---

[7] Augustine, *Confessions,* Book X, chapter xxvii.

www.ingramcontent.com/pod-product-compliance
Lightning Source LLC
LaVergne TN
LVHW041343080426
835512LV00006B/592